T0016551

"A great introduction or refresher on living ~~ing~~ relationship with Jesus. Biblically grou~~nd~~ idly applied to real life, it will help readers to get going or keep going in following Jesus."

GRAHAM BEYNON, Pastor, Grace Church, Cambridge; Director of Independent Ministry Training, Oak Hill College, London

"This is the discipleship course I've been waiting for! Simple but well-written, with thought-provoking discussion questions and illustrations, this guide to life in Christ will encourage and equip new believers—and those who have followed Jesus for years—to live out a joyful, hopeful, purposeful life with him."

CAROLYN LACEY, Author, *Extraordinary Hospitality (For Ordinary People)* and *Say the Right Thing*

"A simple, winsome and helpful tool for discipling new Christians (and rediscipling older ones) in our modern world. It's a great blend of accessible biblical material, robust theology and clear questions that both comfort and confront. And it's written in an engaging style, with examples from everyday life that ring true. Life seems complex in the 21st century, but as Tim Chester shows, everything we need for discipleship—a life with Jesus in the modern world—is available to us in the gospel. I can think of any number of groups to use this with."

STEPHEN MCALPINE, National Communicator, City Bible Forum, Australia; Author, *Being the Bad Guys*

"The Christian life is a privilege, but one we often find deeply confusing. We easily lose sight of who Jesus has made us to be, how he wants us to mature, and how he has called us to honour him in our communities, and churches and behind closed doors. In these short, simple studies we have help. Through story, engagement with Scripture, prose and personal reflection, Tim Chester provides biblical fuel for growth and, in the process, helps new and mature believers alike to live more wholeheartedly for Christ."

HELEN THORNE, Director of Training and Resources, Biblical Counselling UK

"This is really refreshing material. Accessible and adaptable, it enables us to see how following Jesus is fleshed out in ordinary life. Through stories and Scripture, we are given a glorious perspective on the gritty practicalities of life in our world. If you ask a Christian friend or your small group to use *Life with Jesus*, I'm sure you'll find that the engaging questions prompt conversations which connect our lives together and with our God. Whether you've been following Jesus for a few weeks or many decades, you will be encouraged to walk more closely with him, for our good and his glory."

JOHN RUSSELL, Lead Minister, Cornerstone Church, Nottingham

"*Life with Jesus* covers the foundations of being a disciple of Jesus in an accessible way. It explains how to know Jesus personally and what it is like to follow him. The structure is helpful, with stories which begin each chapter elegantly linked to a Bible study, followed by teaching and application questions. The book would work well in one-to-one or small-group settings. It's terrific, and I will certainly use it with athletes and coaches."

GRAHAM DANIELS, General Director, Christians in Sport

LIFE WITH JESUS

Life with Jesus
© Tim Chester 2023

Published by:
The Good Book Company

thegoodbook.com | thegoodbook.co.uk
thegoodbook.com.au | thegoodbook.co.nz | thegoodbook.co.in

thegood**book**
COMPANY

Unless indicated, all Scripture references are taken from the Holy Bible, New International
Version. Copyright © 2011 Biblica, Inc. Used by permission.

Tim Chester has asserted his right under the Copyright, Designs and Patents Act 1988 to be
identified as author of this work.

ISBN: 9781784988234 | Printed in India

Design by Ben Woodcraft

CONTENTS

INTRODUCTION

disciple n. 1. One of Christ's personal followers.

What does it mean to be a disciple of Jesus? What does it mean to follow him?

That's what this course is about. You may have just become a Christian and want to know what happens next. You may have been a Christian for more years than you care to remember and simply want a refresh.

We're going to explore what it looks like to follow Jesus and how Jesus enables us to keep going. We'll see that Jesus gives us a new life with a new hope in a new family. Indeed, being a Christian doesn't start with what we do, but with what Jesus has done for us. Then we'll look at how knowing Jesus changes our view of God and our obedience to God. Our connection to Jesus gives us a power for life and a hope for the future. We'll explore how we can remain connected to Jesus through the Bible, prayer and the Lord's Supper. Finally we'll look at the impact that knowing Jesus makes to key areas of our lives. It all adds up to a compelling life that will attract other people to Jesus.

You can use this course on your own, with another person or in a small group—there's a Leader's Guide at the back which gives some ideas on how to use it. If you're new to Christianity, it would be good to read it with someone who's been a Christian for a while, someone who knows the ropes. Each session is designed so it can be done in about an hour if you've read the chapter ahead of time, or a bit more if you come without any preparation. This means you could work through each session one-to-one in a lunch break or with a small group in an evening. Don't feel you have to answer every question. It's much better to focus in on what seems most relevant to you or your group.

Following Jesus is not always easy. It can cut against the grain of our selfish desires. We can find ourselves out of step with the world around us. But it is the good life. It's a life that is full and rich, a life with purpose, a life with God, and a life that leads to eternal life.

PART ONE

A new life

The Christian message is the good news that Jesus has risen, conquering sin and death—and that now Jesus invites us to share his new life.

It's a life of forgiveness because sin has been overcome and it's a life of hope because death has been defeated.

It's also life in a new family, the church.

Being a Christian doesn't start with what we do; it starts with what Jesus has done for us.

1. GOSPEL

We share the
victory of Jesus

JACK'S STORY

It felt a bit weird telling Jordan what had happened. Jack was fit to burst with excitement, but at the same time he wasn't sure how Jordan would react. It was Monday morning and they were driving to the school where they both worked.

"I went to church again yesterday," said Jack.

"Oh yeah," said Jordan, showing more interest in the traffic.

Jack explained what the preacher had said and described the invitation to become a Christian. "And that's what I did. I prayed to God. Just like that. It felt great."

"Wow, that's quite something," said Jordan. "So what happens now?"

Jack wasn't sure what to say. "We take a left down the High Street—like we always do."

Jordan laughed. "Very funny. But seriously. What does becoming a Christian actually mean? Are you going to become a monk or something?"

"No, of course not. At least, I don't think so. I don't know."

Jack thought to himself. What *had* happened?

COLOSSIANS 1 v 15–23

Read the following extract from the Bible. They are the words of the apostle Paul. Mark any phrases you find striking or puzzling.

15 The Son is the image of the invisible God, the firstborn over all creation. 16 For in him all things were created: things in heaven and on earth, visible and invisible, whether thrones or powers or rulers or authorities; all things have been created through him and for him. 17 He is before all things, and in him all things hold together. 18 And he is the head of the body, the church; he is the beginning and the firstborn from among the dead, so that in everything he might have the supremacy. 19 For God was pleased to have all his fullness dwell in him, 20 and through him to reconcile to himself all things, whether things on earth or things in heaven, by making peace through his blood, shed on the cross.

21 Once you were alienated from God and were enemies in your minds because of your evil behaviour. 22 But now he has reconciled you by Christ's physical body through death to present you holy in his sight, without blemish and free from accusation— 23 if you continue in your faith, established and firm, and do not move from the hope held out in the gospel. This is the gospel that you heard and that has been proclaimed to every creature under heaven, and of which I, Paul, have become a servant.

1. How do these verses describe Jesus, the Son of God?

2. How does verse 21 describe people *before* they become Christians?

3. How does verse 22 describe people *after* they become Christians?

4. What has Jesus done to bring about this change?

5. How does this passage answer Jack's question?

WE SHARE THE VICTORY OF JESUS

The Christian message is *good news*—that's what the word "gospel" means. Imagine a country at war. Finally a messenger arrives: "Good news—our army has triumphed". The Christian message is the good news that Jesus has triumphed.

To understand who the winners and losers are in the victory of Jesus, we need to wind the clock back to the beginning of history. God is for ever a community of three persons: Father, Son and Holy Spirit—full of life and love. In his love, God made a world of beauty and wonder to share his joy. But humanity rejected God's rule or "kingdom". We wanted to be gods of our own lives. We still do. This is what the Bible calls "sin". Our rebellion has put us on a collision course with God.

Good news and bad news

Jesus, the Son of God, came to restore God's kingdom. That's good news because God's kingdom is a kingdom of life, freedom and joy (as Jesus repeatedly demonstrated during his life on earth). But there's a problem. The coming of God's kingdom is not good news if you're a rebel against God—and that includes all of us. For rebels, the coming of God's kingdom means defeat and judgment.

The wonderful twist

The wonderful twist in the story is that Jesus didn't judge God's enemies (that's still to come). Instead, God's judgment fell upon Jesus himself at the cross. Jesus died under God's judgment *in our place* so we could go free. He died so that the coming of God's kingdom might be good news rather than bad news. Three days later God raised him to life again as the beginning of God's new people and the Lord of God's restored kingdom.

THINK IT THROUGH

1. What is the impact for us of the death of Jesus?

2. What is the impact for us of the resurrection of Jesus?

First and foremost

This means that, first and foremost...

- Christianity is *not* a project to build a better world—that's the job of Jesus, though we do get to join in.

- Christianity is *not* about trying to be good—though it does transform us.

- Christianity is *not* a new set of opinions—though it does make us see many things differently.

- Christianity is *not* becoming religious—though it will make us want to pray.

First and foremost, Christianity is about Jesus. It tells the story of his birth, life, death and resurrection. It's the good news that Jesus has defeated sin and death. As a result, Jesus gives forgiveness and eternal life to his people. Instead of being enemies of God, we've now been reconciled to God: "Once you were alienated from God and were enemies in your minds because of your evil behaviour. But now he has reconciled you by Christ's physical body through death to present you holy in his sight, without blemish and free from accusation" (v 21-22).

One day Jesus will come again to this earth to judge humanity. But Christians don't need to fear that day, because through Jesus we're now "free from accusation". So, for Christians the return of Jesus will mean the restoration of God's kingdom in a world made new—a world without suffering and sadness.

THINK IT THROUGH

3. How has becoming a Christian changed the way you think or feel or behave?

4. What are some of the ways you need to continue to change?

ACTION POINTS

Head: Ask a couple of people in your church what changed when they started following Jesus.

Heart: Are there guilty or shameful memories that haunt you? Imagine them being washed away by the work of Jesus.

Hands: You've left behind your old allegiance to sin and started a new life with Jesus. Is there an area of your life where you still need to switch allegiance?

NOTES

2. GRACE

We enjoy the welcome of Jesus

ALYSSA'S STORY

"I'm definitely going to try harder from now on."

It had been Alyssa's first visit to church. Now she and Molly were walking home together.

"What do you mean?" asked Molly.

"I love it. I love it all. Going to church. Hearing about God. Jesus. A life of love. So I'm going try harder. Then maybe I can be a Christian like you."

Like me? If only you knew, thought Molly. To Alyssa she said, "You can't make yourself a Christian by doing good or being religious. You just need to trust in Jesus."

"What? Surely there's more to it than that. What about loving your neighbour and going to church? Surely they're important."

"Well, yes," said Molly. She hesitated. "And no." How was she going to explain it?

EPHESIANS 2 v 1-10

Read the following extract from the Bible. They are the words of the apostle Paul. Mark any phrases you find striking or puzzling.

> [1] As for you, you were dead in your transgressions and sins, [2] in which you used to live when you followed the ways of this world and of the ruler of the kingdom of the air, the spirit who is now at work in those who are disobedient. [3] All of us also lived among them at one time, gratifying the cravings of our flesh and following its desires and thoughts. Like the rest, we were by nature deserving of wrath. [4] But because of his great love for us, God, who is rich in mercy, [5] made us alive with Christ even when we were dead in transgressions—it is by grace you have been saved. [6] And God raised us up with Christ and seated us with him in the heavenly realms in Christ Jesus, [7] in order that in the coming ages he might show the incomparable riches of his grace, expressed in his kindness to us in Christ Jesus. [8] For it is by grace you have been saved, through faith—and this is not from yourselves, it is the gift of God—[9] not by works, so that no one can boast. [10] For we are God's handiwork, created in Christ Jesus to do good works, which God prepared in advance for us to do.

1. What's the plight of all people before they become Christians, according to verses 1-3?

2. What has God done, according to verses 4-7?

3. What's the reason we've been saved, according to verses 8-10? Which comes first—God's grace or our good works?

4. Where do good works fit into the story of our salvation?

5. How might this passage help Molly respond to Alyssa's questions?

WE ENJOY THE WELCOME OF JESUS

Christianity is the good news that Jesus has triumphed over sin and death. But where do you and I fit in? How do we get to share in the victory of Jesus?

Repentance and faith

Jesus began his ministry on earth by saying, "The kingdom of God has come near. Repent and believe the good news!" (Mark 1 v 15). A person becomes a Christian when they respond to the good news by repenting and believing. "Repentance" literally means "turning around"—away from life without God and towards life with God. "Believing" or "faith" means agreeing with the message, but also entrusting yourself to Jesus as your Saviour. Some people can remember the day when they first did this; for others it took place over a period of time. What matters is that we've entrusted ourselves to Jesus.

Coming with empty hands

Faith is like holding out empty hands to God. We don't say, "Look at my good works, my religious activity, my respectable life".

Instead our hands are empty to receive salvation as a gift. After all, human beings are too messed up to be able to earn anything from God. We were a bit like zombies—dead souls walking about in living bodies (Ephesians 2 v 1). We had neither the capacity nor inclination to please God. Of course, we did many good things—we loved our families and gave to charity. But the fundamental orientation of our lives was away from God.

Fortunately, the story didn't end there. "But because of his great love for us, God, who is rich in mercy, made us alive with Christ even when we were dead in transgressions—it is by grace you have been saved" (v 4-5). God didn't wait for us to make the first move. If he had done, he would still be waiting! God took the initiative in history when he sent Jesus to take the wrath we deserved in our place so we could be forgiven. And God also took the initiative in your life when he sent his Spirit to give you spiritual life.

THINK IT THROUGH

1. If you think your relationship with God depends on good works, what's likely to happen when you have a bad day? How does being saved by grace change this?

2. Even when we grasp that we're saved by grace, in practice we can still act as if God's acceptance depends on our behaviour. Can you think of examples of this?

We don't get God's blessing because we give to the needy or pray regularly or know the Bible or volunteer for charity. These are all great things to do. But they don't make us more acceptable to God. That's because we can't be any more acceptable than we already are through Jesus! Take a moment to let this sink in. Despite all the wrong things you may have done today, if you're a Christian you're as acceptable to God as if you'd had a perfect day. You may not feel that, but then it's not your feelings that make you acceptable to God! Whether you feel it or not, you're close to God through Jesus. That's because what matters is Jesus, and his worth never fluctuates.

God's grace followed by our good works

Christ has saved us "to do good works, which God prepared in advance for us to do" (v 10). Many people assume good works are what make you a Christian, as if our good works earn God's grace. But that's the wrong way round. First comes God's grace and only then are we set free to do good works. God welcomes us into his family and then gives us good works to do.

Think of it like this. Apples don't give life to a branch. But they are a sign that a branch has life. Life comes first and then apples. In the same way, good works don't make us spiritually alive, but they are the fruit of genuine spiritual life. Good works may help us enjoy our relationship with God, but they don't create that relationship. It's Jesus who connects us to God, and that connection can't be any stronger than it already is.

THINK IT THROUGH

3. How does salvation by grace change the way we view ourselves? How does it change the way we view other people?

4. Christians need to avoid both "legalism" (thinking our good works earn God's blessing) and "lawlessness" (thinking grace means we can get away with sin). When are you most likely to fall into each of these traps?

ACTION POINTS

Head: Verse 10 says, "We are God's handiwork, created in Christ Jesus to do good works, which God prepared in advance for us to do". What good works do you think God has prepared for you to do?

Heart: Does your guilt ever make you reluctant to pray? Imagine yourself sat next to Christ in heaven, with his arm round your shoulders (Ephesians 2 v 6).

Hands: Find three ways to do good this week.

NOTES

3. CHURCH

We belong to the family of Jesus

JACK'S STORY

Tyrone slumped on the sofa, got out his phone and called Jack.

"Hi Jack. It's Tyrone. You ok? We missed you at home group."

"Oh, yeah. Sorry about that. By the time I got home from work I was exhausted."

Tell me about it, thought Tyrone.

"To be honest," said Jack, "I'm not sure about church. I mean, I get Jesus—I really do. I believe that he's the real thing—that my sin is forgiven and I know God. But do I really need to come to church? Surely I can read my Bible and pray at home."

On another day Tyrone might have been straight in there with an answer. But the truth was, it was a question he'd been asking himself too. Church had begun to feel like one demand on top of another. What was he going to say to Jack?

COLOSSIANS 3 v 1–17

Read the following extract from the Bible. They are the words of the apostle Paul. Mark any phrases you find striking or puzzling.

¹ Since, then, you have been raised with Christ, set your hearts on things above, where Christ is, seated at the right hand of God. ² Set your minds on things above, not on earthly things. ³ For you died, and your life is now hidden with Christ in God. ⁴ When Christ, who is your life, appears, then you also will appear with him in glory.

⁵ Put to death, therefore, whatever belongs to your earthly nature: sexual immorality, impurity, lust, evil desires and greed, which is idolatry. ⁶ Because of these, the wrath of God is coming. ⁷ You used to walk in these ways, in the life you once lived. ⁸ But now you must also rid yourselves of all such things as these: anger, rage, malice, slander, and filthy language from your lips. ⁹ Do not lie to each other, since you have taken off your old self with its practices ¹⁰ and have put on the new self, which is being renewed in knowledge in the image of its Creator. ¹¹ Here there is no Gentile or Jew, circumcised or uncircumcised, barbarian, Scythian, slave or free, but Christ is all, and is in all.

¹² Therefore, as God's chosen people, holy and dearly loved, clothe yourselves with compassion, kindness, humility, gentleness and patience. ¹³ Bear with each other and forgive one another if any of you has a grievance against someone. Forgive as the Lord forgave you. ¹⁴ And over all these virtues put on love, which binds them all together in perfect unity.

¹⁵ Let the peace of Christ rule in your hearts, since as members of one body you were called to peace. And be thankful. ¹⁶ Let the message of Christ dwell among you richly as you teach and admonish one another with all wisdom through psalms, hymns, and songs from the Spirit, singing to God with gratitude in your hearts. ¹⁷ And whatever you do, whether in word or deed, do it all in the name of the Lord Jesus, giving thanks to God the Father through him.

1. What are we called to do in verses 5-10? What might this look like for you?

2. What should the church be like, according to verses 11-15?

3. Consider the attitudes and actions to which we're called in verses 12-15. Can you think of examples of these from the life of your church?

4. How do we help one another grow as Christians, according to verses 16-17?

5. How might this passage help Tyrone respond to Jack?

WE BELONG TO THE FAMILY OF JESUS

When I used to go to watch my local football team, it was easy to spot the home supporters—they were the ones wearing red and white. Fans express their allegiance by wearing the colours of their team. Paul uses the image of a change of clothes to describe what happens when someone becomes a Christian: "You have taken off your old self with its practices and have put on the new self, which is being renewed in knowledge in the image of its Creator" (v 9-10).

We've removed our "old self" just as if we had taken off a dirty set of clothes. It's literally "the old humanity". Human beings were made to live in relationship with God and one another, but sin messed that up in a big way, which is why our world is so full of conflict (v 8). But our humanity is being restored in the church through Christ. We've *put on* a new humanity in Christ. The old divisions of the old humanity no longer count, because Christ has united us (v 11).

Paul calls us "God's chosen people, holy and dearly loved" (v 12). It's language that was used to describe God's people in the Old Testament. Now it's describing Christians. The Bible story is not simply the story of how God saves individuals. It's the story of God's people. You and I are saved when by faith we become part of God's people—the people for whom Christ died. So, we're saved into a shared life. Paul describes us as "members of one body" (v 15). It doesn't really matter whether you see yourself as a hand, an ear or a little toe—the point is we belong together and we need one another.

THINK IT THROUGH

1. What differences do you see between the way people in the wider world relate to one another and the way people in your church relate to one another?

2. What are you doing to participate in the life of your church? Is there something more you could do?

We grow together

Paul presents a glorious vision of the church as God's new humanity, but he's also realistic. He knows that life in a local church can sometimes feel a bit pedestrian or even fraught. So he mixes grand descriptions of who we are in Christ with exhortations to put that reality into practice. If church life was always sweetness and light, then Paul wouldn't have to urge us to clothe ourselves with compassion, kindness, humility, gentleness, patience, forbearance and forgiveness (v 12-13)!

Growing as a Christian is not a solo project. It means growing as a member of the community of Christ. That means less anger, rage, malice, slander and filthy language (v 8); and it means more compassion, kindness, humility, gentleness, patience, forbearance and forgiveness (v 12-13). It means growing with your brothers and sisters into a community that is full of love and peace, so that together you display the glory of Jesus (v 14-15).

We help one another grow

Christ has given your local church to you. It's his gift to you to help you grow as a Christian. The church is the community which will teach you more about Jesus and keep reminding you what matters. This is not just about giving information. The preaching of God's word backed up by the worship of the church fuels our passion for Jesus (v 16).

Think of yourself as a piece of coal on fire for Jesus. In the middle of a fireplace, surrounded by other blazing coals, a piece of coal happily remains red hot. But take a piece of coal out of the fire and it soon loses its heat. It's the same with Christians. Take a Christian out of a local church for any length of time and they're likely to lose their passion—the fire goes out. But in the midst of a living church our passion for Jesus is much more likely to remain red hot.

So, why should you be part of a local church? First, there's the *identity reason*. You've been saved into the community of Christ. This is who we are—the family of God. Second, there's the *practical reason*. Your church has been given to you by Christ as the place where you can survive and thrive as a Christian.

THINK IT THROUGH

3. What's been your experience of other people helping you grow as a Christian?

4. What could you do this week to encourage another Christian or help them become more like Jesus?

ACTION POINTS

Head: How might belonging to the church family change the way you think about your time or money?

Heart: Is there someone to whom you could or should show compassion, kindness, humility, gentleness, patience, forbearance or forgiveness this week?

Hands: See if you can encourage three Christians this week by thanking them for the way they serve in your church.

NOTES

PART TWO

A changed perspective

Jesus gives us a new outlook on life.

He changes our perspective on God. Before knowing Jesus, obeying God seemed to be a daunting and even miserable prospect. But now we see God as a loving Father. He is a good God and obeying him is a good life.

Jesus also changes our perspective on life. We now view everything in the light of the eternal life that Jesus promises.

So, our connection to Jesus gives us new power for a life of service and a new hope to endure suffering.

4. OBEDIENCE

Jesus gives us a new view of God

JACK'S STORY

Jack had stopped swearing pretty much overnight and giving up porn had been easier than he thought it would be. There was no doubt that becoming a Christian had changed his life. But anger was still a big issue. He still found it tough not to let his emotions spiral out of control.

"It's not what we do that matters," his Christian friends had told him. "It's all about what Christ has done for us."

I get that, thought Jack. *But if it's all grace, grace, grace, why do I need to obey God's law?* Besides which, it wasn't straightforward. What was he supposed to do when his temper started rising? How could he switch it off?

ROMANS 8 v 12-16

Read the following extract from the Bible. They are the words of the apostle Paul. Mark any phrases you find striking or puzzling.

> *¹² Therefore, brothers and sisters, we have an obligation—but it is not to the flesh, to live according to it. ¹³ For if you live according to the flesh, you will die; but if by the Spirit you put to death the misdeeds of the body, you will live.*
>
> *¹⁴ For those who are led by the Spirit of God are the children of God. ¹⁵ The Spirit you received does not make you slaves, so that you live in fear again; rather, the Spirit you received brought about your adoption to sonship. And by him we cry, "Abba, Father." ¹⁶ The Spirit himself testifies with our spirit that we are God's children.*

1. How do these verses describe God and our relationship with him?

2. What does the Holy Spirit do, according to these verses? How does he change the way we view God?

3. How will you live if you see yourself as a slave, with God as your master?

4. How will you live if you see yourself as a child, with God as your Father?

5. How does this passage answer Jack's questions?

JESUS GIVES US A NEW VIEW OF GOD

Nothing matters more than the way you think about God. If you think of God as a tyrant, then you'll keep him at arm's length or you'll feel like a slave. God doesn't want us to live like that, so he sent his Spirit to help us recognise that he is actually a loving Father (v 14-16). We're united to Jesus by faith, and so the relationship Jesus has with God the Father *by nature* is now the relationship we have *by adoption*. It's so amazing that we would never believe it were it not for the fact that "the Spirit himself testifies with our spirit that we are God's children" (v 16).

This changes everything. God is King, but his rule is a rule of love. God's first words to humanity were: "You are free". "You are free to eat from any tree in the garden; but you must not eat from the tree of the knowledge of good and evil" (Genesis 2 v 16-17). That one restriction gave humanity an opportunity to trust God.

We often assume freedom involves having lots of choices. But true freedom is the capacity to be the best you can be and enjoy what's best for you. Freedom for a fish is not the choice to jump out of the water—that's not freedom, but death. That's because fish thrive in water. Likewise, freedom for human beings is not the choice to be bad—that's not true freedom, but slavery and death. That's because human beings thrive under God's rule of love. God's law might once have felt like a cage, hemming us in. But now we realise it is more like a skeleton, holding us up, enabling us to be truly human and humane.

The miserable lies of sin

Satan came to the first man and woman in the form of a serpent, and portrayed God as a tyrant—restricting our potential, spoiling our fun, holding us back. We believed that lie and decided we were better off without God. That lie still shapes the way people think of God. Underneath every temptation is the lie that we're better off without God. But that's never true.

The rest of the Bible is the story of God showing us that his rule is in fact a loving rule that brings liberty and life. Jesus said he "did not come to be served, but to serve, and to give his life as a ransom for many" (Mark 10 v 45). Far from demanding more from us, Jesus gave his life for us.

The liberating truth of God

God's laws are not arbitrary, nor are they designed to spoil our fun. They're a description of a life of love and freedom. It's true that sometimes we'll find obeying God's law hard work. But the problem is not that God's law is unreasonable, but that we are! If you think you know better than God, then you'll resent his law. But once you see God as a Father, you'll welcome his rule and want to obey his law (Romans 8 v 15).

THINK IT THROUGH

1. How do you view God and his laws? (By "his laws" I mean his will revealed in the Bible.)

2. How should your adoption by God change these assumptions?

So, we fight temptation through faith in the truth. Take Jack's struggle with anger. Suppose a colleague lets Jack down and now Jack's about to blow.

- Jack might be angry because he likes being in control. The truth is that God is in control, and we can entrust ourselves to his care.

- Jack might be angry because his reputation has been jeopardised. The truth is that God's opinion is the only opinion that really matters.

- Jack might be desperate to prove himself and fears his colleague's action will reflect badly on him. The truth is that Jack is a child of God by grace, so he doesn't need to find identity in his work.

Being ruthless with temptation

Romans 8 v 12-13 say that we now have "an obligation": to "put to death the misdeeds of the body". This means ruthlessly saying no to temptation. Obeying God can be tough. It goes against the grain of our old sinful instincts. It can put us out of step with everyone around us. But if we're ever tempted to doubt the goodness of God, we just need to think of Jesus. The cross is the great demonstration that God's intentions for us are good—which means that obeying him will lead to a satisfying life. Remembering this truth helps us say no to temptation. Never forget that we fight temptation "by the Spirit" (v 13). God gives us his Spirit to empower us and inspire us, and to remind us of his fatherly love.

THINK IT THROUGH

3. What might it mean for you to be ruthless with temptation?

4. What truths could you turn to when you find yourself resenting God or his law?

ACTION POINTS

Head: Ask a couple of people in your church what they enjoy about being a Christian.

Heart: Do you ever resent obeying Jesus? Think of him offering himself on the cross and tell yourself his intentions for you are always good.

Hands: Is there some aspect of God's law (his will revealed in the Bible) that you've been reluctant to obey? How can you put that right today?

NOTES

5. UNITED

Jesus gives us a new power for life

ALYSSA'S STORY

Alyssa had been so excited when she'd first become a Christian. It was amazing to think of God as her Father. She loved praying. Wow—what a privilege it was to talk to God! And she loved discovering one amazing thing after another when she read her Bible. She wanted to tell everyone she met about Jesus.

But she soon discovered that people weren't always interested in listening. Even her Christian friends had got a bit fed up. What was new to her wasn't new to them. Then a new job had meant a longer commute and that meant less time to read her Bible. She tried reading on the bus, but it was hard to concentrate.

Today she'd got home from work and realised it was home-group night. Her heart sank. All she wanted to do was slump on the sofa and watch TV.

"How's it going?" asked Molly later that evening as they walked home together.

"I don't know," said Alyssa. There was a pause. Then she asked, "Why does being a Christian suddenly feel like hard work?"

JOHN 15 v 1–17

Read the following extract from the Bible. They are the words of Jesus, speaking to his disciples on the night before he died. Mark any phrases you find striking or puzzling.

> *¹ I am the true vine, and my Father is the gardener. ² He cuts off every branch in me that bears no fruit, while every branch that does bear fruit he prunes so that it will be even more fruitful. ³ You are already clean because of the word I have spoken to you. ⁴ Remain in me, as I also remain in you. No branch can bear fruit by itself; it must remain in the vine. Neither can you bear fruit unless you remain in me.*
>
> *⁵ I am the vine; you are the branches. If you remain in me and I in you, you will bear much fruit; apart from me you can do nothing. ⁶ If you do not remain in me, you are like a branch that is thrown away and withers; such branches are picked up, thrown into the fire and burned. ⁷ If you remain in me and my words remain in you, ask whatever you wish, and it will be done for you. ⁸ This is to my Father's glory, that you bear much fruit, showing yourselves to be my disciples.*
>
> *⁹ As the Father has loved me, so have I loved you. Now remain in my love. ¹⁰ If you keep my commands, you will remain in my love, just as I have kept my Father's commands and remain in his love. ¹¹ I have told you this so that my joy may be in you and that your joy may be complete. ¹² My command is this: love each other as I have loved you. ¹³ Greater love has no one than this: to lay down one's life for one's friends. ¹⁴ You are my friends if you do what I command. ¹⁵ I no longer call you servants, because a servant does not know his master's business. Instead, I have called you friends, for everything that I learned from my Father I have made known to you. ¹⁶ You did not choose me, but I chose you and appointed you so that you might go and bear fruit—fruit that will last—and so that whatever you ask in my name the Father will give you. ¹⁷ This is my command: love each other.*

1. Think about the image of a vine and branches. In what way is Jesus like a vine? In what way are we like branches?

2. Look for all the times Jesus uses the phrase "remain in me" in verses 1-8. What does he say in each case?

3. What will happen if we remain in Jesus, according to verses 1-8?

4. What does it mean to remain in Jesus, according to verses 9-13?

5. How might this passage help Molly respond to Alyssa's frustrations?

JESUS GIVES US A NEW POWER FOR LIFE

What's the secret to being a successful Christian? Here's what Jesus said: "Remain in me, as I also remain in you. No branch can bear fruit by itself; it must remain in the vine. Neither can you bear fruit unless you remain in me" (John 15 v 4). When you become a Christian, you're united to Christ. In fact, the Bible rarely uses the term "Christian". Much more often it speaks of those who are "in Christ".

But what does it mean to be "in Christ" and to "remain in Christ"? It might sound a bit weird.

A relational connection

Jesus calls his disciples friends (v 14). To remain in Christ is to remain friends with him. With friends we keep in touch; with Jesus that means hearing his voice in the Bible and talking to him in prayer. With friends we say sorry when we let them down; with Jesus that means confessing our sin. With friends we spend time on shared passions; with Jesus that means loving what he loves.

A spiritual connection

Being in Christ is also a spiritual connection. That's another way of saying that it's a connection made *by the Holy Spirit*—a connection that's living and life-giving (v 4-5). Just as life flows from a vine to its branches, so life flows from Christ to us through the Holy Spirit. And just like a branch connected to a vine, this connection to Jesus means we bear fruit. For Christians that means "love, joy, peace, forbearance, kindness, goodness, faithfulness, gentleness and self-control" (Galatians 5 v 22-23).

Think of it like this. Most of us have relationships we find energising. When we spend time with these people, we come away feeling buoyed up or inspired. Our relationship with Jesus is a super-energising relationship. Spending time with him inspires us or reassures us or excites us. That's partly because he's such an inspirational person. But it's also because our connection with him is supernatural. Jesus is full of life and some of that life flows to us when we spend time with him.

THINK IT THROUGH

1. How do you stay in touch with your friends?

2. How might you apply the same principles to your relationship with Jesus?

So, how do we remain connected to Jesus?

1. We listen to what Jesus says

Remaining in Jesus includes ensuring that "my words remain in you" (v 7). That means hearing the Bible preached week by week and reading it for ourselves day by day.

2. We ask for what Jesus offers

Jesus gives us a wonderful promise: "Ask whatever you wish, and it will be done for you" (v 7). It's not an invitation to indulge our whims—to ask for a Porsche or a beach-ready body! Jesus says, "This is to my Father's glory, that you bear much fruit" (v 8). Jesus is inviting us to ask God to help us bear fruit that will honour him.

3. We love what Jesus loves

"If you keep my commands," says Jesus, "you will remain in my love" (v 10). Jesus has one particular command in mind. "My command is this:" he says in verse 12, "love each other as I have loved you". It's only one command, but it pretty much covers everything! All God's laws are essentially explanations of how we can best love other people (Romans 13 v 8-10; Galatians 5 v 14).

Following Jesus can be hard going. Reading the Bible takes time and sometimes we'd rather do something else. Loving other people often involves sacrifice. If we neglect our relationship with Jesus, then being a Christian can feel like a bunch of obligations. Then it becomes a slog. What energises us is our connection to Jesus. So when service feels like a burden, it's time to reconnect with Jesus. "I have told you this," says Jesus, "so that my joy may be in you and that your joy may be complete" (v 11).

THINK IT THROUGH

3. What might it mean for you to love what Jesus loves?

4. What steps could you take if serving Jesus begins to feel like a slog or a burden?

ACTION POINTS

Head: The Christian life is a life Jesus gives rather than a task to accomplish. How does that change your perspective on the coming week?

Heart: Does serving Jesus ever feel like a slog? Take some time to reconnect with him as a friend.

Hands: Our connection to Jesus means we bear the fruit of the Spirit, which are "love, joy, peace, forbearance, kindness, goodness, faithfulness, gentleness and self-control" (Galatians 5 v 22-23). Pick one of these fruits and pray each day that you'll bear more of this fruit in your life.

NOTES

6. SUFFERING

Jesus gives us a new hope for the future

ALYSSA'S STORY

"I thought being a Christian would be easy, but sometimes it's really tough."

Alyssa and Molly were sitting in their favourite coffee shop. Alyssa kept stirring her tea—even though she didn't take sugar.

"Do you want to talk about it?" said Molly.

"My mother's illness—it's tough. Seeing her suffer is so hard. I've asked God to cure her, but nothing's happened. What's God doing?"

Molly was trying to work out what to say when Alyssa continued.

"One of my friends says I need more faith. Does that mean it's my fault my mum's not getting better? Or is it God's fault? I don't know what to think."

ROMANS 8 v 17–30

Read the following extract from the Bible. They are the words of the apostle Paul. Mark any phrases you find striking or puzzling.

17 Now if we are children, then we are heirs—heirs of God and co-heirs with Christ, if indeed we share in his sufferings in order that we may also share in his glory.

18 I consider that our present sufferings are not worth comparing with the glory that will be revealed in us. 19 For the creation waits in eager expectation for the children of God to be revealed. 20 For the creation was subjected to frustration, not by its own choice, but by the will of the one who subjected it, in hope 21 that the creation itself will be liberated from its bondage to decay and brought into the freedom and glory of the children of God.

22 We know that the whole creation has been groaning as in the pains of childbirth right up to the present time. 23 Not only so, but we ourselves, who have the firstfruits of the Spirit, groan inwardly as we wait eagerly for our adoption to sonship, the redemption of our bodies. 24 For in this hope we were saved. But hope that is seen is no hope at all. Who hopes for what they already have? 25 But if we hope for what we do not yet have, we wait for it patiently.

26 In the same way, the Spirit helps us in our weakness. We do not know what we ought to pray for, but the Spirit himself intercedes for us through wordless groans. 27 And he who searches our hearts knows the mind of the Spirit, because the Spirit intercedes for God's people in accordance with the will of God.

28 And we know that in all things God works for the good of those who love him, who have been called according to his purpose. 29 For those God foreknew he also predestined to be conformed to the image of his Son, that he might be the firstborn among many brothers and sisters. 30 And those he predestined, he also called; those he called, he also justified; those he justified, he also glorified.

1. How do verses 19-21 describe the present experience of the created world?

2. According to verses 17-18, 21 and 23, what will happen to creation and Christians in the future?

3. How do verses 18, 23 and 25 describe Christians' present experience?

4. According to verses 26-27, what's the Holy Spirit doing when we find life tough?

5. How does this passage answer Alyssa's questions?

JESUS GIVES US A NEW HOPE FOR THE FUTURE

Christianity is the good news of the victory of Jesus over sin and death. Hurray! So why is life often tough? Where's the victory when you've been made redundant or diagnosed with cancer?

The answer is that God is waiting before he restores creation. He's waiting so that people have the opportunity to turn to him in faith and repentance. In the meantime, here are three wonderful truths that help us cope when suffering comes our way.

God will end suffering (v 18-25): One day "creation itself will be liberated from its bondage to decay" and Christians will enjoy "the redemption of our bodies" (v 21, 23). God will renew all things and there will be no more sickness, suffering, sin or death.

God is with us in our suffering (v 26-27): God the Son has experienced what it is to be human. Jesus knows what it's like to be weary, frustrated, bereaved, misunderstood and betrayed. And now his Spirit "helps us in our weakness" (v 26).

God uses suffering to make us like Jesus (v 28-30): God uses "all things"—including suffering—for our good (v 28-29). Suffering deepens our character, makes us depend more on Jesus, and focuses our attention on eternal glory. We can't always see how this process is happening, but we can be confident that God's purposes for us are good because he's given us his Son (v 32, 37).

THINK IT THROUGH

1. How have you known Christ's presence and the Spirit's help in suffering?

2. How have you seen God using suffering to make you more like Jesus?

Suffering followed by glory

Some Christians want resurrection glory now. They expect God to make them healthy and wealthy here and now. But the Bible says we're not there yet. The world has not yet been made new. In the meantime, we must be patient (v 24-25). So Christians suffer along with everyone else. In fact, Christians sometimes face additional suffering because of the hostility of people who reject Christ.

In this way we follow the pattern of Christ himself—the pattern of suffering followed by glory. "We share in his sufferings in order that we may also share in his glory" (v 17). Our lives now are shaped by the cross—we suffer like Jesus and we sacrifice like Jesus. This is how Jesus himself defines what it means to be a Christian: "Whoever wants to be my disciple must deny themselves and take up their cross daily and follow me" (Luke 9 v 23). We're called to live a life of love in which we die to self and put others first. It's a beautiful life to see and it's a beautiful life to live.

Power to sacrifice

But sacrificial love and self-denial don't come easily. They keep bumping into our old selfish instincts. That's why the Holy Spirit gives us resurrection power. The same power that reached into the grave and brought Jesus back from physical death has reached into your life and brought you back from spiritual death. Resurrection life circulates around your soul, just as blood circulates around your body. Jesus rose again in victory, and he shares that victory with his people. If you think this makes us sound like superheroes with power fizzing through our veins, then you are not far off!

But this power doesn't make us immune to suffering—like someone on an airport travelator gliding past people struggling with suitcases. That's not real life, and it's not what God promises. Instead, we have resurrection power *so we might suffer with Christ and love like Christ*. We have resurrection life now so we can die to self.

So, life can be tough. But can trouble, hardship or persecution ever separate us from Christ's love? Here's God's answer: "No, in all these things we are more than conquerors through him who loved us. For I am convinced that neither death nor life, neither angels nor demons, neither the present nor the future, nor any powers, neither height nor depth, nor anything else in all creation, will be able to separate us from the love of God that is in Christ Jesus our Lord" (v 37-39).

THINK IT THROUGH

3. What would you say to someone who claims we can be healed if we just have enough faith?

4. Can you see ways in which the cross and resurrection are shaping your life?

ACTION POINTS

Head: Having right expectations makes a big difference when suffering comes. What can Christians expect in the present? In the future?

Heart: "We share in his sufferings in order that we may also share in his glory" (v 17). Next time you face hostility, rejoice that sharing Christ's suffering is a sign that you'll share his glory.

Hands: What might it mean for you to die to self and put others first in the next ten minutes? The next ten hours? The next ten days? The next ten months?

NOTES

PART THREE

A real connection

Christianity is not simply a set of ideas or rules for life. First and foremost, it's a living relationship with the living God. And God has given us the Bible, prayer and the Lord's Supper to maintain our connection to him.

In the Bible we can hear God's voice; in prayer we can seek his help; and in the Lord's Supper we can know his love.

7. BIBLE

We can hear
God's voice

JACK'S STORY

"I get why the Bible is important," said Jack. "You know, it's God's word and all that. But it's hard going sometimes. So I started thinking, what I need is some kind of summary of the Bible—everything the Bible teaches, made short and simple. *The Bible for Dummies*, perhaps. Something like that must exist, surely. I could read it and that would save me the bother of ploughing through the Bible itself. So, is there a book like which you can recommend?"

Tyrone put down the really rather excellent guide to discipleship they were reading together and wondered where to begin.

2 PETER 1 v 12-21

Read the following extract from the Bible. They are the words of the apostle Peter. Mark any phrases you find striking or puzzling.

> *¹² So I will always remind you of these things, even though you know them and are firmly established in the truth you now have. ¹³ I think it is right to refresh your memory as long as I live in the tent of this body, ¹⁴ because I know that I will soon put it aside, as our Lord Jesus Christ has made clear to me. ¹⁵ And I will make every effort to see that after my departure you will always be able to remember these things.*

> *¹⁶ For we did not follow cleverly devised stories when we told you about the coming of our Lord Jesus Christ in power, but we were eyewitnesses of his majesty. ¹⁷ He received honour and glory from God the Father when the voice came to him from the Majestic Glory, saying, "This is my Son, whom I love; with him I am well pleased." ¹⁸ We ourselves heard this voice that came from heaven when we were with him on the sacred mountain.*

> *¹⁹ We also have the prophetic message as something completely reliable, and you will do well to pay attention to it, as to a light shining in a dark place, until the day dawns and the morning star rises in your hearts. ²⁰ Above all, you must understand that no prophecy of Scripture came about by the prophet's own interpretation of things. ²¹ For prophecy never had its origin in the human will, but prophets, though human, spoke from God as they were carried along by the Holy Spirit.*

1. When Peter says "we" in verses 16-18, he's referring to the apostles who wrote the New Testament. What does Peter say in these verses about the record of Jesus in the New Testament?

2. In verses 19-21, Peter talks about the prophets who wrote the Old Testament. What does Peter say in these verses about the promises of Jesus in the Old Testament?

3. What was the relationship between the human authors and the Holy Spirit in the writing of the Bible?

4. What is Peter's main concern, according to verses 12-15? How might this concern affect the way we read the Bible?

5. How might this passage help Tyrone respond to Jack's concerns?

WE CAN HEAR GOD'S VOICE IN THE BIBLE

Jesus has given us a number of things to help us live and grow as Christians. They're sometimes called "the means of grace". That's because they're not skills we need to master. They're gifts through which Christ nourishes and nurtures us. Being a Christian is never an achievement we have to accomplish; it is always a gift we receive through God's grace. But we do have to make use of these means of grace. Imagine someone providing you with nourishing meals day after day. They do all the hard work, but you still need to eat the food. Those meals won't do you any good if the food stays on the plate. In the same way, we need to use these gifts if we want to grow. In the next three sessions we'll look at three key means of grace: prayer, the Lord's Supper and, first, the Bible.

A reliable word

Peter says, "We did not follow cleverly devised stories when we told you about the coming of our Lord Jesus Christ in power, but we were eyewitnesses of his majesty" (v 16). He's talking about what would later be known as the New Testament. The New Testament is the eyewitness account of Jesus and the early church. Then Peter talks about the Old Testament—what he calls "the prophetic message"—spoken by prophets "as they were carried along by the Holy Spirit" (v 19, 21).

The Bible is the word of God because the Spirit of God ensured that what was written was exactly what God intended. Every part of the Bible has two authors. There's the human author with their own distinctive style and personality. But there's also the divine author. So we read the words of Moses or David or Isaiah or Peter, but simultaneously they're also the words of God. That means what we read is "completely reliable" (v 19). The Bible is true and trustworthy in all that it affirms. God intends to communicate to us in the Bible—and God is good at what he does!

THINK IT THROUGH

1. How should the fact that the Bible was written by human authors to particular people facing particular challenges affect the way we read it?

2. How should the fact that the Bible is written by God affect the way we read it?

A living and life-giving word

The divine authorship of the Bible also means it's powerful. At one point Jesus said, "The words I have spoken to you—they are full of the Spirit and life" (John 6 v 63). Just as the Spirit spoke through the *writers* of the Bible, so he continues to speak to *readers* of the Bible. As a result, the words of the Bible give life to dead hearts. The Holy Spirit sustains us through God's word.

A contemporary word

Because the words of the Bible come in the power of the Spirit, they're also *contemporary* words. "For everything that was written in the past was written to teach us, so that through the endurance taught in the Scriptures and the encouragement they provide we might have hope" (Romans 15 v 4). The Bible was written *for you*. Most books of the Bible were first written for a specific situation, so it helps to keep the original readers in mind. But the Bible always transcends its original context to help you endure, to encourage you and to give you hope.

A Christ-centred word

When the relevance to you is hard to spot, remember that the Bible is all about Jesus. Jesus once said to some religious leaders: "You study the Scriptures diligently because you think that in them you have eternal life. These are the very Scriptures that testify about me" (John 5 v 39-40). It's easy to see how the New Testament is about Jesus. But the Old Testament, too, is full of promises and pictures of Jesus.

A relational word

Above all, what we hear in the Bible are words of love from our Saviour. As you read the Bible, Jesus is speaking to you—right here, right now. Peter says, "I will always remind you" and "refresh your memory" so you will "always be able to remember" (v 12-15). Although sometimes we'll learn new things when we read the Bible, most of the time we're being reminded of what we already know— just like a wife hearing words of reassurance from her husband. We come with our fears, our shame and our doubts, and Christ speaks words of comfort to our battered hearts and words of life to our weary souls.

THINK IT THROUGH

3. What are the key influences on your thinking and your desires? What could you do to minimise unhelpful influences and maximise Bible-shaped influences?

4. Can you think of a recent occasion when Christ spoke to you through the Bible to bring life, reassurance, challenge or comfort?

ACTION POINTS

Head: Are there parts of the Bible you find hard to accept as reliable? Find someone with whom you can talk through your questions, or read a book on the subject, such as *Can I Really Trust the Bible?* by Barry Cooper.

Heart: Next time you read your Bible, begin by praying: "Lord Jesus, please speak to me today through your word to comfort or challenge me."

Hands: If you don't already read your Bible each day, make a start this week. If you're not sure what to do, then get hold of some Bible-reading notes, or read a passage and then respond to each verse in turn with praise and prayer. You might want to begin with Mark's Gospel.

NOTES

8. PRAYER

We can seek
God's help

ALYSSA'S STORY

"I hope I can be a great pray-er like you one day," said Alyssa.

Molly was a bit taken aback. She'd never thought of herself as a great pray-er.

"Could you teach me?" Alyssa continued. "I'd love to know the secret. Are there breathing exercises or something? And how do you know what to say? Whenever I try to pray I quickly run out of things to say or I get distracted. I start thinking about the things I've got to do that day. God must think I'm pretty pathetic! But perhaps with some practice I can get better. So, what's the secret?"

MATTHEW 6 v 5-13

Read the following extract from the Bible. They are the words of Jesus. He is speaking to his disciples. Mark any phrases you find striking or puzzling.

> *5 And when you pray, do not be like the hypocrites, for they love to pray standing in the synagogues and on the street corners to be seen by others. Truly I tell you, they have received their reward in full. 6 But when you pray, go into your room, close the door and pray to your Father, who is unseen. Then your Father, who sees what is done in secret, will reward you. 7 And when you pray, do not keep on babbling like pagans, for they think they will be heard because of their many words. 8 Do not be like them, for your Father knows what you need before you ask him.*
>
> *9 This, then, is how you should pray:*
> *"Our Father in heaven,*
> *hallowed be your name,*
> *10 your kingdom come,*
> *your will be done,*
> *   on earth as it is in heaven.*
> *11 Give us today our daily bread.*
> *12 And forgive us our debts,*
> *   as we also have forgiven our debtors.*
> *13 And lead us not into temptation,*
> *   but deliver us from the evil one."*

1. Look for the phrase "do not be like" in verses 5 and 8. What are the wrong ways to pray (see also verse 7)?

2. How does Jesus describe God in these verses?

3. What difference does this make to the way we pray?

4. Work through each phrase in verses 9-13. What are we asking for in each case?

5. How might this passage help Molly respond to Alyssa's questions?

WE CAN SEEK GOD'S HELP IN PRAYER

"This, then, is how you should pray," says Jesus in Matthew 6 v 9. This is his prayer manual, and it boils down to one simple principle: remember that God is your Father.

Jesus starts by telling us how *not* to pray. First, we're not to be like hypocrites who pray simply to impress other people (v 5-6). When Jesus says they get their reward, he's being ironic. They get what they want—other people are impressed. But they don't get *God's* blessing. True Christians come as children to their Father, so our prayers don't have to be impressive or eloquent. Just think how young children ask their parents for things—that's our model. What matters is that we're confident that God is our Father and he loves his children.

Second, we're not to be like pagans who "think they will be heard because of their many words" (v 7-8). In reality, the true God is too powerful to be nagged into submission. But he's also too loving to need manipulating. He's a loving Father who knows what we need before we ask.

So, what's the technique that will make our prayers effective? There isn't one! That's the point. What counts are not the words you use or how long you pray. What counts is the love of your heavenly Father!

THINK IT THROUGH

1. How should thinking of God as our Father shape our attitude to prayer?

2. How do you feel about praying aloud with other people? If it makes you nervous, what truths might help you overcome this fear?

Our Father in heaven

Just as Jesus is God's child by nature, so we're now God's children by grace. That means Christians share the same access to God that Jesus himself enjoys. That's why the model prayer that Jesus gives us—what we know as "the Lord's Prayer"—starts with a reminder that we're praying to our Father.

Hallowed be your name

"Hallow" is an old word for "holy". So to pray "hallowed be your name" is to pray for God's reputation. You could apply this in your own life and ask for help to reflect God's holiness in the way you live. Or you could apply this to the church and ask for people to be saved so that they start honouring God's name.

Your kingdom come

Later on in Matthew's Gospel, Jesus tells this parable: "The kingdom of heaven is like a mustard seed, which a man took and planted in his field. Though it is the smallest of all seeds, yet when it grows, it is the largest of garden plants and becomes a tree, so that the birds come and perch in its branches" (Matthew 13 v 31-32). At the moment most people ignore God. But God's kingdom is growing as the "seed" of his word is proclaimed and people submit to him in faith. And one day God's kingdom will be the only show in town. So we pray that we would obey God more, that other people would become Christians, and that Christ would return in victory.

Your will be done, on earth as it is in heaven

Jesus himself prayed these words on the night before his crucifixion (Matthew 26 v 42). He naturally recoiled from the horror of what the cross would involve, but in love he submitted to God's plan. So to pray "your will be done" is to submit to whatever God has chosen for us.

Give us today our daily bread

In Matthew 6 Jesus also reminds us that our Father feeds the birds and clothes the flowers (v 25-30). "So do not worry, saying, 'What shall we eat?' or 'What shall we drink?' or 'What shall we wear?' For the pagans run after all these things, and your heavenly Father knows that you need them. But seek first his kingdom and his righteousness, and all these things will be given to you as well" (v 31-33). Jesus invites us to bring our worries to God so we can focus on serving him.

Forgive us our debts, as we also have forgiven our debtors

By "debts" Jesus means our sins—the obligations of love and obedience that we've failed to give to God. Christians have been forgiven their past, present and future sins. So our status before God isn't dependent on regular acts of penitence. But confessing our sin restores our sense of closeness to God. It also reminds us that God's mercy to us is meant to flow out in mercy towards others.

Lead us not into temptation, but deliver us from evil

The word "temptation" means both being enticed to sin and being tested by difficult circumstances. It's not a request to escape this sort of thing, but that we'll be kept safe through temptation. It's a request to keep obeying and trusting Jesus, even when it's tough.

THINK IT THROUGH

3. How does the content of the Lord's Prayer compare with that of your prayers?

4. Think about some things you're praying for at the moment. How might the Lord's Prayer shape the way you pray for these things?

ACTION POINTS

Head: Do you struggle to find time to pray, or to get on with it when you do have time? What does this reveal about your view of God?

Heart: Prayer is not a skill to master, but a gift to enjoy. What difference might this make to your attitude to prayer?

Hands: Each day this week, pray through the Lord's Prayer line by line, turning each phrase into specific requests.

NOTES

9. COMMUNION

We can know
God's love

JACK'S STORY

Jack slumped on the sofa. "Where are you when I need you, Jesus?" he said.

He'd had a rubbish day at work. He'd had to sort out a crisis and so he ended up leaving late. On the way home he got stuck in traffic. Now he felt tired and deflated. He couldn't be bothered to cook a proper meal so he'd just made himself some toast.

Part of the problem was he knew it had all been his fault. He'd lost his temper and now he felt guilty. *What kind of a Christian am I?* he thought.

"Jesus, I could really do with some kind of sign right now," he said aloud. "Something to let me know you're here for me."

1 CORINTHIANS 10 v 16-17 AND 11 v 23-26

Read the following extract from the Bible. They are the words of the apostle Paul. Mark any phrases you find striking or puzzling.

> 10 v 16 *Is not the cup of thanksgiving for which we give thanks a participation in the blood of Christ? And is not the bread that we break a participation in the body of Christ?* 17 *Because there is one loaf, we, who are many, are one body, for we all share the one loaf ...*

> 11 v 23 *For I received from the Lord what I also passed on to you: the Lord Jesus, on the night he was betrayed, took bread,* 24 *and when he had given thanks, he broke it and said, "This is my body, which is for you; do this in remembrance of me."* 25 *In the same way, after supper he took the cup, saying, "This cup is the new covenant in my blood; do this, whenever you drink it, in remembrance of me."* 26 *For whenever you eat this bread and drink this cup, you proclaim the Lord's death until he comes.*

1. Paul is describing what we call "Communion", "the Lord's Supper" or "the Eucharist". What does the bread represent, according to 10 v 16-17 and 11 v 24?

2. What does the wine represent, according to 10 v 16 and 11 v 25?

3. Look at 10 v 17. How does the Lord's Supper bring us together as a local church?

4. Jesus says we share bread and wine "in remembrance of me" (11 v 24-25). What are we remembering?

5. How does the Lord's Supper meet Jack's need?

WE CAN KNOW GOD'S LOVE IN COMMUNION

Notes on the fridge. Writing on your hand. A knotted handkerchief. How do you remember things? Communion is an enacted memory aid. "Do this in remembrance of me," says Jesus (11 v 24). Of course it's not that we can't recall who Jesus is or what he's done. But we easily get distracted. Sometimes all we can see are our problems. Communion helps us take a step back and see the bigger picture. And what we see is God's love displayed in the gift of his Son. At other times our heads fill with doubt. Perhaps we feel we've let God down and so we wonder if he still accepts us. Communion is Christ's gift to remind us that he's covered all our sins. That's why Paul says we "proclaim the Lord's death" in Communion (11 v 26).

Jesus could have given us a form of words by which to remember him. He could have said, *Say this in remembrance of me*, or *Think this...* But he knows how battered by life we can be. So he gives bread and wine as physical reminders of his love. The bread and wine are tangible expressions of his promise and presence.

THINK IT THROUGH

1. Why do you think Jesus gives us bread and wine in Communion rather than simply communicating through words?

2. What would you miss if your church stopped celebrating Communion?

The promise of Christ in bread and wine

"This cup is the new covenant in my blood," says Jesus, according to 11 v 25. The account in Matthew's Gospel adds a little more: "Then [Jesus] took a cup, and when he had given thanks, he gave it to them, saying, 'Drink from it, all of you. This is my blood of the covenant, which is poured out for many for the forgiveness of sins'" (Matthew 26 v 27-28).

Jesus promises "the forgiveness of sins". But he doesn't just promise this—he makes a covenant. A covenant is a kind of legal contract. When we make a contract today we normally put a signature at the bottom to confirm our commitment to the promises listed above. Jesus expresses his commitment in the wine of Communion—it's his signature at the bottom of the contract. Every time you receive the Communion wine, Jesus is affirming afresh his commitment to forgive your sins.

Think what this means to Jack. He's racked by guilt because of the way he lost his temper and perhaps damaged Christ's reputation. But when he receives Communion, Jesus is reassuring Jack that he's forgiven. We *hear* the promises of Jesus in the gospel, but we also get to *see* those promises and *taste* them in bread and wine.

The presence of Christ in bread and wine

The bread and wine are not only signs of Christ's promise; they're also signs of his presence. Of course God is present everywhere. But throughout the Bible, God promises to be with his people in a special way—to comfort, guide and protect them. We particularly experience this presence when we gather together as God's people. We hear the voice of God when his word is preached. Perhaps we feel his presence as we sing together. But above all we enjoy Christ's presence in Communion. Paul describes it as "the Lord's table" (1 Corinthians 10 v 21). Jesus himself is the host when we celebrate Communion. He invites us to eat with him as a sign of his love.

This doesn't mean that the bread and wine literally transform into the physical body and blood of Jesus. At the first Christmas, Jesus became truly human with a real human body. At the first Easter, that body physically rose from the dead and later ascended. So, the body of Jesus is now in heaven. If his body appeared every time Communion was celebrated, then Jesus would no longer be truly human with a real human body.

But, through the Holy Spirit, Jesus is genuinely present with us. He may not be physically present, but he's spiritually present. Not only that; the presence of Jesus takes tangible form in the bread and wine. Jesus knows how fragile and frail we are, so he gives bread and wine as signs or tokens of his presence.

Think what this means to Jack. He longs for a sign that Christ is there for him. Bread and wine are that sign. A good husband will tell his wife that he loves her, and Christ tells us that he loves us in the gospel message. But a good husband will also hug his wife as a physical demonstration of his commitment to her. Communion is Christ's reassuring hug.

THINK IT THROUGH

3. How might you pray as you prepare to receive Communion?

4. Can you think of times when you've found Communion especially comforting or nourishing?

ACTION POINTS

Head: What should you be thinking as you receive bread and wine?

Heart: Next time you participate in Communion, receive the bread and wine as gifts from Jesus, physical expressions of his love for you.

Hands: Think about your current spiritual needs and identify how Christ meets those needs. Then think of a way the Lord's Supper symbolises the way Christ meets your need.

NOTES

PART FOUR

A compelling lifestyle

Knowing Jesus leads to a changed life. And the biggest changes often come in our attitude to money, sex and power.

Jesus expects us to be generous with our money while offering us contentment.

He expects us to use authority to serve others—something he himself modelled when he died for us.

And he expects us to be sexually pure while offering us a life that is rich and full.

It all adds up to a compelling lifestyle. Christians attract people to Jesus through our lives and our words.

10. MONEY

Jesus enables us to lead a contented life

ALYSSA'S STORY

"Can you give me some advice?" said Alyssa. She and Molly had just finished their weekly Bible study. "It's nothing to do with Christianity. It's about something else."

"Sure. Go ahead," said Molly, wondering what was coming next.

"I've maxed out my credit card again," said Alyssa. "I'm not sure what to do. I need to get my spending under control. The truth is, most of it isn't really stuff I need. When I'm feeling a bit down I tend to cheer myself up with a bit of the old 'retail therapy'. Can you give me any pointers?"

Molly thought for a moment. She was thinking whether there was anyone in the church who might be able to give financial advice. But she was also wondering whether this issue might actually have rather a lot to do with Christianity.

MATTHEW 6 v 19-24

Read the following extract from the Bible. They are the words of Jesus. He is speaking to his disciples. Mark any phrases you find striking or puzzling.

> *19 Do not store up for yourselves treasures on earth, where moths and vermin destroy, and where thieves break in and steal. 20 But store up for yourselves treasures in heaven, where moths and vermin do not destroy, and where thieves do not break in and steal. 21 For where your treasure is, there your heart will be also.*
>
> *22 The eye is the lamp of the body. If your eyes are healthy, your whole body will be full of light. 23 But if your eyes are unhealthy, your whole body will be full of darkness. If then the light within you is darkness, how great is that darkness!*
>
> *24 No one can serve two masters. Either you will hate the one and love the other, or you will be devoted to the one and despise the other. You cannot serve both God and Money.*

1. What do you think Jesus means by treasure on earth and treasure in heaven?

2. Why should we make treasure in heaven our priority?

3. In verses 22-23, Jesus says that what we look at will shape our priorities. What do you look at that makes you want to store up treasure on earth? What do you look at that makes you want to store up treasure in heaven?

4. What do you think it looks like to serve money (v 24)?

5. How might this passage help Molly respond to Alyssa's issues?

JESUS ENABLES US TO LEAD A CONTENTED LIFE

Three of the big challenges in life are money, sex and power. They're all powerful forces that shape people's lives. We can use them in good and beautiful ways. But they also have the potential to derail our relationship with Jesus. We'll look at sex in the next chapter. Here we consider money and (more briefly) power.

Jesus once told a story about a man who found some treasure in a field. The man sold everything he owned to buy the field and enjoy the treasure (Matthew 13 v 44). People must have thought the man was crazy—selling everything to buy a scrappy piece of land. But Jesus says he did so "in his joy". Of course he did; he was getting something much more valuable. The point is that Christians have found an amazing treasure. We've found forgiveness, freedom, eternal life. Above all, we've found Jesus. And so *in our joy* we make sacrifices to follow Jesus—because he's worth more than anything else.

A new attitude to money

"If only I had more money," many people think, "then I would be happy". But it doesn't work because we were made for more—we were made for God. And in the end you can't take money with you. So Jesus tells us to store up treasure in heaven rather than on earth (Matthew 6 v 19-20).

We know it makes sense. But money still has a powerful pull on our hearts. Jesus says: "No one can serve two masters. Either you will hate the one and love the other, or you will be devoted to the one and despise the other. You cannot serve both God and Money" (v 24). There's nothing wrong with money itself—it can do a lot of good. But money can be like a god. We think it will rescue us from our problems and make us happy. So we make sacrifices for it. This is what makes it so dangerous. It can become a rival to Jesus in our lives.

Be grateful

"Godliness with contentment is great gain," says 1 Timothy 6 v 6. Instead of pursuing wealth, we're to pursue contentment. But how can we find contentment? One simple thing we can do is to be grateful. It's easy to focus on what we lack. We imagine that if only we could get that promotion, buy that car, fix up our house, then we'd be happy. And all the time God has blessed us in a thousand wonderful ways. The act of giving thanks redirects our thinking from what we lack to what we've received, and from the gift to the Giver.

Be generous

God encourages us to be generous with our money, time, homes and possessions.

The people of Israel were encouraged to give a tenth of their income. The standard for Christians is the generosity of Jesus: "See that you also excel in this grace of giving … For you know the grace of our Lord Jesus Christ, that though he was rich, yet for your sake he became poor, so that you through his poverty might become rich" (2 Corinthians 8 v 7, 9). Giving money is an important way to support Christian work and care for those in need. But it also benefits us:

being generous liberates us from the power of money and helps us appreciate the generosity of God.

THINK IT THROUGH

1. What's our culture's attitude to money and possessions?

2. How is our attitude as Christians supposed to be different?

A new attitude to power

Knowing Jesus also transforms our attitude to authority. Satan persuaded the first man and woman to think of God as a tyrant (as we saw in session 4). Ever since, we've been suspicious of authority. But Jesus is a model of using authority to serve others (Mark 10 v 42-45).

Be willing to submit to power

It's right to resist injustice. If we ever have to choose, then "we must obey God rather than humans beings" (Acts 5 v 29). But our default should be to submit to authority—in the home, the workplace, the church and in society. Because of human pride and selfishness, authority structures no longer work perfectly—we know that all too well. But God still uses them for our good (Romans 13 v 1-7; 1 Peter 2 v 13 – 3 v 7; Hebrews 13 v 17).

Use authority to serve

When you have authority, you should use it like Jesus did—to serve others. You may still have to make tough decisions; sometimes unpopular decisions. But you will want to use your authority to serve other people rather than to serve yourself (Ephesians 5 v 22 – 6:9; 1 Peter 5 v 1-4).

THINK IT THROUGH

3. What might it mean for you to submit to authority in the home, the workplace, society or the church?

4. What might it mean for you to use authority to serve others in the home, the workplace, society or the church?

ACTION POINTS

Head: What did you do last week to store up treasure on earth? What will you do this week to store up treasure in heaven?

Heart: Each day this week, spend some time giving thanks to God for the good things in your life—everything from a piece of toast to the promise of eternal life.

Hands: If you're not already giving regularly to the work of your church, talk to someone about the best way to do this.

NOTES

11. SEX

Jesus enables us to lead a full life

JACK'S STORY

"Don't get me wrong," said Jack, "I love being a Christian—I love Jesus. But living without sex is hard; really hard. Everywhere you look there's something that stokes the fires!"

"Tell me about it," said Tyrone.

"It's ok for you—you're happily married."

"Yes, but it's still a struggle not to fantasise about other women."

Jack raised an eyebrow. He looked doubtful. But he carried on regardless: "I mean, what if I never get married? What kind of a life is that?"

Tyrone was sympathetic. How could he offer Jack some hope?

1 CORINTHIANS 6 v 9-20

Read the following extract from the Bible. They are the words of the apostle Paul. Mark any phrases you find striking or puzzling.

9 Or do you not know that wrongdoers will not inherit the kingdom of God? Do not be deceived: Neither the sexually immoral nor idolaters nor adulterers nor men who have sex with men 10 nor thieves nor the greedy nor drunkards nor slanderers nor swindlers will inherit the kingdom of God. 11 And that is what some of you were. But you were washed, you were sanctified, you were justified in the name of the Lord Jesus Christ and by the Spirit of our God.

12 "I have the right to do anything," you say—but not everything is beneficial. "I have the right to do anything"—but I will not be mastered by anything. 13 You say, "Food for the stomach and the stomach for food, and God will destroy them both." The body, however, is not meant for sexual immorality but for the Lord, and the Lord for the body. 14 By his power God raised the Lord from the dead, and he will raise us also. 15 Do you not know that your bodies are members of Christ himself? Shall I then take the members of Christ and unite them with a prostitute? Never! 16 Do you not know that he who unites himself with a prostitute is one with her in body? For it is said, "The two will become one flesh." 17 But whoever is united with the Lord is one with him in spirit.

18 Flee from sexual immorality. All other sins a person commits are outside the body, but whoever sins sexually, sins against their own body. 19 Do you not know that your bodies are temples of the Holy Spirit, who is in you, whom you have received from God? You are not your own; 20 you were bought at a price. Therefore honour God with your bodies.

1. Paul quotes two slogans from the culture of his first readers: "I have the right to do anything" and "Food for the stomach and the stomach for food" (i.e. sex is just a bodily appetite like hunger). Do you hear anything like this today?

2. How do verses 12-13 counter these attitudes?

3. What do verses 14-20 say about our bodies?

4. How does becoming a Christian heal the effects of sexual sin and pain, according to verse 11?

5. How does this passage help to answer Jack's questions?

JESUS ENABLES US TO LEAD A FULL LIFE

God's intention is for marriage to be a life-long union between a man and a woman. Quoting from the story of the first marriage, Jesus says: "Haven't you read ... that at the beginning the Creator 'made them male and female,' and said, 'For this reason a man will leave his father and mother and be united to his wife, and the two will become one flesh'? So they are no longer two, but one flesh. Therefore what God has joined together, let no one separate" (Matthew 19 v 4-6).

Sometimes people talk about "a marriage made in heaven". But in fact every marriage is made in heaven. It's God who joins a man and woman together through the covenant commitments they make in the wedding ceremony and through the powerful bonding that takes place during sex.

So marriage is the God-given context for sex. This is why God rules out pre-marital and extra-marital sex. Indeed, Jesus says: "I tell you that anyone who looks at a woman lustfully has already committed adultery with her in his heart" (Matthew 5 v 28). That rules out porn and sexual fantasies. To emphasise how important this is, Jesus adds, "If your right eye causes you to stumble, gouge it out and throw it away" (v 29).

Sex is a gift that binds couples together

It's not that God is anti-sex. Quite the opposite. God is very much pro-sex. After all, he invented it! The issue is that sex is too precious and too powerful to be misused. Sex is really good at its job, which is binding couples together in life-long union. But this power wreaks havoc when it's misused. Outside of marriage, sex is like gluing two pieces of wood together and then tearing them apart. It's not the glue that breaks, but the wood. The result is like a splintering of souls and that is not easily healed. Something of your self is left behind. So when God says that sex belongs only in marriage, it's not to stop us having fun, but to stop us getting hurt. It's not because sex is bad. It's because sex is too life-changing to be unleashed without life-long commitment.

THINK IT THROUGH

1. How would you respond if someone asked you why God restricts sex to marriage?

2. What attitudes to sex do you see in the world around you? Can you spot ways these attitudes have unhelpfully influenced you?

Sex is a gift that points us to God's love

It's not easy to follow a life of sexual purity, because it's so out of step with our culture. And some of us may have to unlearn deeply embedded patterns of behaviour. But it can lead to a life of satisfaction and fulfilment. That's because sex is designed by God to be a sign of God's own giving of himself to us so that we might be one with him. The Bible says that marriage and sex are a picture of Christ's relationship with his people (Ephesians 5 v 31-32). At the cross Christ gave himself in love to save people, to take the judgment we deserve, to cleanse us and make us beautiful. And Christ commits himself to us *totally*. He's made a covenant (like a marriage covenant) to love us and care for us.

So the number one reason God invented sex was to reveal his passion for his people.

• All the hurt you feel around sex is like the hurt God feels at our unfaithfulness.

• All the joy you feel around sex is like Christ's joy in his people.

• All the sacrifices you make are like the sacrifice Jesus made for us.

Our culture constantly tells us that to be whole or worthwhile we need to have sex or romance. But the Bible says that singleness as well as marriage is good (1 Corinthians 7 v 38). Sex does its job beautifully when it helps bind couples together in life-long union. Whether we're married or unmarried, we can wrongly suppose that sex or romance or porn will give us a sense of meaning, potency, respect, belonging or identity. But we mustn't make sex do a job it wasn't designed to do. Sex is great, but it's not a substitute for God. You can cope with the disappointments of married life—because you have

God. You can have a complete life, a full life, a fulfilled life without sex—because you have God. Exhibit A is Jesus himself. Jesus was the perfect human being while remaining single.

We're all broken, and for many of us that means our sexuality is broken in some way or other. Some have been hurt by sex; others have caused hurt. Many of us carry the scars of shame or guilt. But there is hope. Talking about people who were once "sexually immoral", the Bible says: "That is what some of you were. But you were washed, you were sanctified, you were justified in the name of the Lord Jesus Christ and by the Spirit of our God" (1 Corinthians 6 v 11).

THINK IT THROUGH

3. What do people seek from sex and romance in addition to physical pleasure? How does Jesus offer something better?

4. What good news does Christianity offer to single people? To those who are in unhappy marriages?

ACTION POINTS

Head: How does the way you think about marriage, singleness or sex need to change?

Heart: What can your experiences of sexual longing or pleasure or betrayal teach you about God's love for you?

Hands: If you've not done so already, consider putting accountability software on your computer and other devices. Accountability software will inform a friend you've chosen if you visit dubious websites.

NOTES

12. WITNESS

Jesus enables us to lead an attractive life

ALYSSA'S STORY

"I told someone about Jesus today," said Alyssa.

"Wow, that's brilliant," said Molly. But one look at Alyssa made it clear that it had not been brilliant.

"What happened?" asked Molly.

"I told my friend Anne that she needed Jesus, that she couldn't sort her life out by herself." There was a pause. "She didn't take it well. She told me not to be so arrogant. But I was only trying to help—she does need Jesus."

"Be patient," said Molly. "Anne may need time to think it through."

But Alyssa was still going. "Then someone else joined the conversation. She asked me whether there were dinosaurs in Noah's ark. I didn't know what to say. I know we're supposed to tell other people about Jesus. But not me—I can't do it."

Molly gave Alyssa a hug while she tried to think of something encouraging to say.

1 PETER 2 v 9-12 AND 3 v 8-16

Read the following extract from the Bible. They are the words of the apostle Peter. Mark any phrases you find striking or puzzling.

> *2 v 9 But you are a chosen people, a royal priesthood, a holy nation, God's special possession, that you may declare the praises of him who called you out of darkness into his wonderful light. 10 Once you were not a people, but now you are the people of God; once you had not received mercy, but now you have received mercy.*
>
> *11 Dear friends, I urge you, as foreigners and exiles, to abstain from sinful desires, which wage war against your soul. 12 Live such good lives among the pagans that, though they accuse you of doing wrong, they may see your good deeds and glorify God on the day he visits us ...*
>
> *3 v 8 Finally, all of you, be like-minded, be sympathetic, love one another, be compassionate and humble. 9 Do not repay evil with evil or insult with insult. On the contrary, repay evil with blessing, because to this you were called so that you may inherit a blessing. 10 For,*
>
> *"Whoever would love life*
>   *and see good days*
> *must keep their tongue from evil*
>   *and their lips from deceitful speech.*
> *11 They must turn from evil and do good;*
>   *they must seek peace and pursue it.*
> *12 For the eyes of the Lord are on the righteous*
>   *and his ears are attentive to their prayer,*
> *but the face of the Lord is against those who do evil."*
>
> *13 Who is going to harm you if you are eager to do good? 14 But even if you should suffer for what is right, you are blessed. "Do not fear their threats; do not be frightened." 15 But in your hearts revere Christ as Lord. Always be prepared to give an answer to everyone who asks you to give the reason for the hope that you have. But do this with gentleness*

and respect, ¹⁶ keeping a clear conscience, so that those who speak maliciously against your good behaviour in Christ may be ashamed of their slander.

1. What do 2 v 11-12 and 3 v 8-12 say about how we're to live?

2. What do 2 v 9 and 3 v 15 reveal about what we're to say?

3. According to 3 v 15-16 what's our attitude to be when we speak about Jesus?

4. According to 2 v 12 and 3 v 14 what responses (good and bad) can we expect when we tell people about Jesus?

5. How might this passage help Molly respond to Alyssa?

JESUS ENABLES US TO LEAD AN ATTRACTIVE LIFE

Christianity is the good news of a wonderful victory and a gracious invitation (as we saw in sessions 1 and 2). Jesus has conquered sin and death, and now he offers forgiveness and eternal life. "News" is something to share with other people; all the more so when it's "*good* news". And the victory of Jesus is the best news possible. No other invitation offers people hope for this life *and* the life to come.

Yet sadly many people don't hear the good news of Jesus as good news. People are often hostile to Jesus and accuse us of being in the wrong (2 v 12). You may sometimes feel like a "foreigner"—an outsider—in your home or workplace (2 v 11).

The reason for this hostility is that people choose self-rule over God's rule. The chances are, you once thought like that. But at some point the Holy Spirit opened your eyes to see the glory and grace of Christ. When that happened, following Christ seemed like a no-brainer—despite the sacrifices it might involve. And the Holy Spirit does the same thing in the lives of other people as the good news of Jesus is proclaimed. It can be our privilege as Christians to see that supernatural work take place before our eyes as we tell other people about Jesus.

We make Jesus known through our lives

Christians are attractive people. Knowing Jesus makes us less self-ish and more loving. While that transformation is far from complete, there is real change and people will notice the difference. We're becoming attractive people—people who attract others to Jesus.

The Bible says: "Live such good lives among the pagans that, though they accuse you of doing wrong, they may see your good deeds and glorify God on the day he visits us" (2 v 12). How do we persuade people? By living good lives and doing good deeds. We're to be ready "to give the reason for the hope that [we] have" (3 v 15). But what is it that's going to prompt people to ask questions about our faith? A life that displays our hope in Jesus.

And you're not on your own. Just before we're told to be ready to give a reason for our hope, we're told: "All of you, be like-minded, be sympathetic, love one another, be compassionate and humble" (3 v 8). The love and unity of your church is a powerful sign of hope. It's often the shared life of the church that gets people asking questions. The chances are that nowhere else in your neighbourhood does such a diverse group of people come together to be family.

So look for opportunities to introduce people to your church family.

THINK IT THROUGH

1. Have you experienced hostility when you've told people about Jesus? How can you respond well when this happens?

2. What opportunities do you have to introduce people to your church family?

We make Jesus known through our words

Attractive lives are important, but they're not enough. People need the good news of Jesus, and by definition "news" is something to declare with words. God has chosen you "that you may declare the praises of him who called you out of darkness into his wonderful light" (2 v 9). You are to "always be prepared to give an answer to everyone who asks you to give the reason for the hope that you have" (3 v 15).

You may not be able to preach a sermon, but you can tell people what Jesus has done for you. Or you can invite them to come to church. Another great thing to do is to invite people to read one of the Gospels, because then they'll meet Jesus himself through the very words of God.

Notice that we're to tell people about Jesus "with gentleness and respect" (3 v 15). It's tempting to feel defensive and so end up getting angry. But it's not our job to win the argument. We're not to manipulate or pressurise people. Our job is simply to speak of Jesus as clearly as we can. The rest we can leave to the Holy Spirit. He's the one who ultimately persuades people to accept the message of Jesus.

Always remember that the good news of Jesus is good news—not bad news. It's the good news of a wonderful victory. Jesus has defeated sin and death to give us forgiveness and eternal life. So Jesus offers hope for this life and the life to come. What's at stake is the glory of Jesus and the eternal future of our friends.

THINK IT THROUGH

3. We're to "be prepared to give an answer … for the hope that [we] have" (3 v 15). What would you say if someone asked you why you have hope for eternal life?

4. Does telling people about Jesus ever make you feel anxious? What truths might help counter this anxiety?

ACTION POINTS

Head: Suppose on Monday morning someone asks about your weekend. Think of a way to talk about what happened at church on Sunday that will point them to Jesus or encourage them to ask more questions.

Heart: People are quick to tell others about what excites them, and their enthusiasm is often infectious. So, think what excites you about Jesus.

Hands: Think of three people you could talk to about Jesus or invite to church. Then pray for an opportunity to talk to them.

NOTES

LEADER'S GUIDE

If you're putting together a piece of self-assembly furniture, then you need to follow all the steps in the right order. If you don't, then you may end up with a door put on the wrong way round. But assembling a disciple of Jesus Christ doesn't work like this! It's a more organic process, and it's a process that ultimately is in God's hands.

A menu not a manual

Because discipleship is an organic process, don't feel you need to follow every step in this course in the right order. Think of the everyday stories, the Bible-study questions, the "Think it through" questions and the action points as items on a restaurant menu rather than a self-assembly manual. They're all optional. You don't have to have a three-course meal just because it's on the menu. In the same way, you don't necessarily need to consider every single question. Instead pick the exercises and questions that are most relevant to you or your group.

Beginning and ending in prayer

Because discipleship is a divine process, you need to pray. This course on its own will not bring growth in Christ. It is God who makes people more like his Son, through his word and by his Spirit. So I suggest you start and end each session in prayer. Start by praying that God would speak to you through the course material. God may teach you new truths, or he may remind you of old truths that you need to hear afresh. And then end by praying that God would help you put into practice what you've learnt or seen afresh.

FOUR SCENARIOS

Here are four scenarios for doing the course and how you might adapt it in each case.

On your own

If you're studying the course on your own then you can work through each chapter at your own pace.

- Reading is not the same as studying. So do pause to consider the introductory story, the Bible-study questions, the "Think it through" questions and the action points. Not all of them will be relevant to you, but don't rush past them and miss what God may be wanting to teach you.

- Although you're studying on your own, it will help if you can find ways to share what you're learning. If something particularly strikes you, then tell a friend or family member. Or share what you've discovered with your small group or pastor. A lesson shared is a lesson strengthened.

- Learning is not the same as growing. Our aim is to not merely expand our knowledge, but to become more like Jesus. So make sure you put your learning into practice, perhaps by using the action points.

A one-to-one get together

This course has been designed to create some structure to a discipleship relationship—a relationship in which a mature Christian helps a newer Christian grow in their faith or where peers help one another grow. You could meet up once a week and discuss one chapter each time.

- Read the content of a chapter aloud when you meet. Start with the introductory story. This usually ends with a "poser" as someone tries to think what to do or say. You could ask one another what you would do or highlight any links to your own experience.

- Then read the Bible extract aloud together and consider some of the questions.

- Next read the main section, pausing to consider any of the "Think it through" questions that seem relevant. If time is short—for example, if you're meeting in a lunch break—then you could each read the chapter beforehand so you can come ready to dive straight into the "Think it through" questions.

- Finally, you could highlight one or two action points before ending in prayer.

A small group
Consider the introductory story together, work through the Bible extract, read the main body of the chapter aloud and then discuss any of the "Think it through" questions that seem interesting or relevant. Groups are likely to spend more time in discussion because there are more potential contributors, so you will either need to select the most appropriate Bible study and "Think it through" questions or allow more time.

A four-session course
The individual chapters are organised into four groups of three, so the material can also be studied as a four-week course. With this option, participants will need to read all three chapters beforehand, looking at the Bible extracts and considering the "Think it through" questions, so that they come prepared. When you meet, you could do a mix of the following in whatever combination best suits your group:

- Open with one of the introductory stories, to get people talking. (Most groups will probably only have time to consider one of these stories.)

- Work through one of the Bible extracts.

- Highlight whatever lessons from the main material in the chapters are most appropriate to your group, and then use a selection of the "Think it through" questions to open up discussion. If you have time, you could do this for each of the three chapters in turn.

• Challenge people to do two or three of the action points before the next session.

COMPANY

BIBLICAL | RELEVANT | ACCESSIBLE

At The Good Book Company, we are dedicated to helping Christians and local churches grow. We believe that God's growth process always starts with hearing clearly what he has said to us through his timeless word—the Bible.

Ever since we opened our doors in 1991, we have been striving to produce Bible-based resources that bring glory to God. We have grown to become an international provider of user-friendly resources to the Christian community, with believers of all backgrounds and denominations using our books, Bible studies, devotionals, evangelistic resources, and DVD-based courses.

We want to equip ordinary Christians to live for Christ day by day, and churches to grow in their knowledge of God, their love for one another, and the effectiveness of their outreach.

Call us for a discussion of your needs or visit one of our local websites for more information on the resources and services we provide.

Your friends at The Good Book Company

thegoodbook.co.uk | thegoodbook.com
thegoodbook.com.au | thegoodbook.co.nz
thegoodbook.co.in